What people are saying about "Not the Bible"

Three times I pleaded with the Lord to take it away from me.
St Paul*

> *O for a thousand tongues to sing this great book's praise*
> Charles Wesley*

This really is the last time I accept anything my wife gives me!
Adam*

> *No book is better than a bad book.*
> Theresa May*

---

* Everything's true about these statements except the quotes.

STILL MORE NOT THE PARABLES OF JESUS

Other books by the author

The Lost Parables Series
The Donkey and the King
Ana and the Prince
The Princess and the Crocodile

Not the Bible Titles
Not the Parables of Jesus
More Not the Parables of Jesus
Not the Parable of the Good Samaritan
Still More Not the Parables of Jesus
Not the Parable of the Lost Sheep (free for subscribers)
Not the Parable of the Rich Fool (subscribers only)
Not the Christmas Story Vol 1 (with devotional)

Christian Parody Titles
Not the Love Dare
Not the Christmas Story: A Comedic Christmas Caper

Christian Satirical News
The Best of the Salty Cee Vol 1

Satirical Publishing Titles
Get 1,000 Readers for Your Self-Published Book

STILL MORE NOT THE PARABLES OF JESUS

Revised Satirical Version (RSV)

John Spencer

Still More Not the Parables of Jesus
Copyright © 2019 John Spencer.

All rights reserved. No part of this book may be copied or reprinted for commercial gain. However, these stories are meant to be shared, used as skits, sermon illustrations, stories for Sunday school or for small group discussion. Individual parables may be reproduced for these purposes, but please honour the effort that went into writing them by referencing their source. For other uses please obtain written permission from the author via his website www.johnspencerwrites.com.

Unless otherwise quoted, all "Not the Bible" quotations are taken from the Revised Satirical Version (RSV) © 2017.

Nothing in this book is intended as a substitute for the Bible. The reader should regularly consult a Bible in matters relating to his/her spiritual development and particularly with respect to any behaviour that may require truth.

The funny thing about this page is that you can write anything and no-one will ever notice. I guess it's kind of like those terms and conditions that everyone clicks "I agree" without ever reading which probably is rather naughty.

Published by:

Kingdom Collective Publishing

Unit 10936, PO Box 6945
London, W1A 6US
kingdomcollectivepublishing@gmail.com

Book and Cover idea by John Spencer, design by Kingdom Covers
Not the Bible icon – design by John Spencer, created by Dalmatirac Design Studio
Editing by Katherine.
ISBN: 978-1-912045-93-8

First Edition: May 2019

Dedication

This one's for the followers on my "Not the Bible" Facebook page.

You make me laugh so much with your responses to my caption competitions and other interactive posts.

It's such a pleasure to serve you and I appreciate you having such low standards that you'd follow my page in the first place.

CONTENTS

What people are saying about "Not the Bible" i
Dedication vii

NOT THE END 3

HAZARD WARNING! 5

NOT THE PARABLES 7

THE PHARISEE AND THE TAX COLLECTOR 9
THE TEN VIRGINS 10
THE GOOD SAMARITAN 12
THE PEARL OF GREAT PRICE 13
THE LOST SHEEP 14
THE PRODIGAL SON 15
THE GREAT BANQUET 17
THE WHEAT AND THE TARES 19
THE SEED GROWING SECRETLY 21
THE LAMP ON A STAND 22
THE LOST COIN 23
THE PERSISTENT WIDOW 24
THE SHEEP AND THE GOATS 25
THE RICH MAN AND LAZARUS 27
THE RICH FOOL 29
THE HIDDEN TREASURE 30
THE TWO SONS 31
THE GOOD SAMARITAN 2 32
PARABLE OF THE TALENTS 33
THE LOST SHEEP 2 35
PARABLE OF THE SOWER 36
THE PEARL OF GREAT PRICE 2 37
THE UNFORGIVING SERVANT 39
THE WEDDING GARMENT 40
PARABLE OF THE TALENTS 2 41
THE PRODIGAL SON 2 43
THE PERSISTENT WIDOW 2 44

- THE SHREWD MANAGER 45
- THE WHEAT AND THE TARES 47
- PARABLE OF THE MUSTARD SEED 48
- THE WICKED TENANTS 49
- THE GOOD SAMARITAN 3 50
- THE SHEEP AND THE GOATS 51

PERFECT PARABLES 53

- THE SHREWD MANAGER 55
- THE RICH MAN AND LAZARUS 57
- THE WEDDING GARMENT 58
- THE TEN VIRGINS 59

POINTLESS PARABLES 61

- THE GREAT BANQUET 63
- THE GOOD SAMARITAN 64
- THE HIDDEN TREASURE 65
- PARABLE OF THE NET 66
- THE WICKED TENANTS 67

THE LOST PARABLES 69

- THE CYST OF SHAME 70

NOT THE BEGINNING 77

- GET BONUS CONTENT 79
- FEEDBACK 80
- ABOUT THE AUTHOR 81
- KEEP IN TOUCH 82
- OTHER BOOKS BY THE AUTHOR 83
- AND FINALLY… 85

NOT the End

A clever section title that makes it sound like it's more important than an introduction.

Hopefully, people might read it which may cut down on the number of angry emails I receive...

Hazard Warning!

- Not suitable for Christians who think Joy is that dear old lady who brings that chicken casserole to the church pot luck.

- May prove flammable to those who miss the all-important word "NOT" in the title.

- May cause a choking hazard if read whilst eating or drinking.

- May cause friends to question your salvation if left on a coffee table.

- May cause disorientation to readers who don't spell words like the beloved Queen.

- May cause a trip hazard for sacred cows, cultural Christianity and pride.

No animals were harmed in the making of this book.

6 | Still More Not the Parables of Jesus

N⊘T
the Parables

Different takes on the parables to restore the wonder, the joy of the Gospel, and the discomfort of discovering what we really believe in our hearts.

Lk 18:9-14
The Pharisee and the Tax Collector

Then he told this parable to those who were confident in their own righteousness and looked down on everyone else.

"Two men went to the Temple to pray; one a Pharisee; the other a tax collector. The Pharisee prayed: 'God, I thank you that I'm not like everyone else, especially not that tax collector over there! For I fast twice a week and give a tenth of all my income.'

But the tax collector stood at a distance, his face in his hands, not daring to look up to Heaven and said, 'God have mercy on me, a sinner.'

I tell you that this tax collector rather than the other went home right with God. For the proud shall be humbled, but the humble shall be raised up."

I bet you're glad you're not like that proud Pharisee, eh?

Mt 25:1-13
The Ten Virgins

The Kingdom of Heaven is like ten girls who took their lamps and went out to meet the bridegroom. Five were foolish, and five were wise. The foolish ones took their lamps but did not take any oil, but the wise ones had oil ready in their lamp's reservoir.

Now the bridegroom was taking his time travelling with his wedding procession, and the girls all grew drowsy and fell asleep. But at midnight there was a shout, 'Here comes the bridegroom! Come and meet him!'

Then the girls awoke and trimmed their lamps. However, since the lamps of the foolish girls had no oil, their flames soon spluttered and went out.

The foolish ones rushed to find the bridegroom's procession and asked, "Could you just wait a moment as we're not ready."

"Very well – go sort yourselves out," they replied.

After purchasing oil from the 24/7 convenience store they returned. "Thank you so much, we're ready now."

The bridegroom's friends again called out with a shout, 'Here comes the bridegroom! Come and meet him!'

And they all joined the procession and went in with him to the wedding banquet.

Therefore you do not need to keep watch, because it is man's destiny to face judgement and if he's not ready he'll be given another chance to sort himself out.

Lk 10:25-37
The Good Samaritan

Jesus replied, "There once was a man travelling from Jerusalem to Jericho. He wasn't attacked by robbers as the Roman Governor had this road patrolled and executed the robbers before he happened along the road. So no one would have their lives inconvenienced by a wounded man lying beside the road."

Mt 13:45-46
The Pearl of Great Price

The Kingdom of Heaven is like a man looking for fine pearls. When he found a merchant selling one of great value, he was overwhelmed by how exquisite it was. And so, he immediately pulled his phone out and took a selfie of himself with the pearl.

As he returned the pearl to the merchant, he thought to himself, "People will never believe the size of this thing! I'll be sure to keep this picture wherever I go as evidence."

With a spring in his step, He set off, rejoicing in his good fortune.

Mt 18:12-14; Lk 15:4-7
The Lost Sheep

What do you think? If a man has one hundred sheep and loses one of them, does he not wait for that sheep to come crawling home apologetically before he accepts it?

In the same way, your Father in heaven won't go looking for you. He expects you to make the first move and it had better be a grovelling one before he considers letting you back in the fold.

Lk 15:11-32
The Prodigal Son

A man had two sons. The younger said to his father, 'Father, give me my share of the estate now, instead of making me wait until you die.' So the Father divided his property.

Soon after, the younger son packed all he had and set off for a distant country. There he squandered his money in wild living until it was all gone. At that time, there was a great famine and he began to starve. The only job he could find was feeding a Gentile farmer's pigs. The boy became so hungry that he wanted to eat the pig swill.

When he finally came to his senses, he said, 'At home, even my father's servants have food to spare; and here, I am starving to death! I will go home to my father and say, 'Father, I've sinned against God and against you. I am no longer worthy to be called your son. Take me on as a hired servant.'

And so, he got up and headed home to his father. But while he was still a long way off, his father saw him and was filled with compassion. He ran to his son, embraced him in his arms, and showered him with kisses. The son began his speech, 'Father, I have sinned against God and against you. I am no longer worthy to be called your son – '

But his father cut him off and said to his servants, 'Quick! Bring the finest robe and put it on him. Put the family ring on his finger and place sandals on his feet. Get the fattened calf and kill it. Let's celebrate and have a feast. For this son of mine was dead and is alive again. He was lost and is found.' So they began to party.

Meanwhile, the older son was in the field working. When he returned home, he heard the music and dancing. Calling to a servant, he asked, 'What's going on?' The servant replied, 'Your brother has come home, and your father has killed the fattened calf in celebration of his safe return.'

The older brother was furious and refused to go in. So his father came out and pleaded with him, but he wouldn't listen. 'All these years I've slaved for you and have done everything you required of me. Yet all that time you never gave me even a young goat for a celebration with my friends. But when this son of yours comes home after throwing away all your money on whores, you celebrate by killing the fattened calf!'

The father replied, 'You're right. Your hard work makes you my favourite son. Tell you what; let's make the party in honour of you.'

Mt 22:1-14; Lk 14:15-24
The Great Banquet

Once, there was a man who prepared a great banquet and then sent out many invitations. When all was ready, he sent his servant to inform the guests that it was time to come. But they all began to make excuses. The first said, 'I apologise, but I've just purchased a field that I need to inspect.'

Another said, 'I apologise, but I've just purchased five pairs of oxen that I need to try out.'

Still another said, 'I am just married, so I need to get home to my wife.'

The servant reported all this to his master. His master was angry and told the servant, 'Quickly, go into the city streets and alleys and invite all the poor, dispossessed, crippled, and blind and bring them here.' But they were offended that they weren't asked first and so refused to come.

So the master said, 'Go into the country lanes and find anybody you can and drag them here so that my house will be full'. But even people in the country know enough not to go with strangers, and they refused the invitation as well. The master was frustrated that none of those he invited would get even the smallest taste of the feast he had prepared.

Mt 13:24-30, 36-43
The Wheat and the Tares

Jesus told them this parable, "The Kingdom of Heaven is like a man who sowed good seed in his field. While he slept, his enemy came and sowed tares in the middle of the corn. When the good seed grew, so did the weeds.

The servants saw this and came to him and said, 'Sir, wasn't that good seed that you sowed in the field? Where did all the weeds come from?'

'An enemy did this,' He replied, and his fury let rip, 'Now my crop is ruined!'

'What shall we do?' asked his servants.

'Pull it all up! I can't even bear to look at the mess.'

So, the enemy won that day, as the wheat was removed and burned along with the weeds."

Later, after the crowds were sent away, the disciples said, "Explain to us the parable of the wheat and the tares."

Jesus answered, "The Son of Man sows the good seed. The field is the world. The good seed stands for the sons of the kingdom, and the tares are the children of the evil one. The enemy who sowed them is the devil."

"So too will the church be completely ruined by the evil one, and the Father will have to start all over again with a new denomination that will be perfect, at least for a while."

Mk 4:26-29
The Seed Growing Secretly

The Kingdom of Heaven is like a seed planted in the ground and grows secretly. Just as the farmer has no idea what is going on underground, so too will you never know what's happening in the Kingdom until you reach Heaven.

Mk 4:21-25; Lk 8:16-18
The Lamp on a Stand

Light is a precious commodity in this dark world. You should guard your little light, so the world doesn't suck all the illumination out of it. Therefore, hide your lamp under a bowl or a bed. Those that do so shall become more holy. Those that don't - what little holiness they might have will be taken away from them.

Lk 15:8-10
The Lost Coin

"Suppose a woman has ten silver coins and loses one. Won't she light a lamp, sweep the house and search every corner of the house until she finds the coin? And when she finds it, won't she call her friends and neighbours to rejoice with her?

So it is with God who..."

At the moment Jesus said this, the Pharisees were outraged and shouted, "How dare you portray God as a woman!" They mobbed him and drove him out of the town and brought him to the edge of the hill on which the town was built, so that they could push him off the cliff. But Jesus walked through their midst and went on his way.

Lk 18:1-8
The Persistent Widow

Jesus told his disciples a parable to show them how to get ahead in this dark world. He said, "There was a judge in a town who did not fear God nor did he care for people. A widow in that town kept at him, 'Grant me justice against my adversary.'

"The judge refused, so the widow didn't pester him further. She prayed for God's judgement over him instead. The judge was struck down by lightning and was replaced by a judge who looked favourably on the widow and immediately granted her request.

"So too should you seek to mete God's judgement out on those who don't give you what you want."

Mt 25:31-46
The Sheep and the Goats

When the Son of Man comes in all his blazing glory together with his angels, he shall sit on his glorious throne. And all the nations shall be gathered before him and he shall separate the people as a shepherd separates the sheep from the goats, putting the sheep to his right and goats to his left.

Then the King will say to those on his right, 'Come, blessed of my Father, take your inheritance – the Kingdom prepared for you from the world's foundation. For I was hungry and you fed me, I was thirsty and you gave me a drink, I was a stranger and you invited me in, I was naked and you clothed me, I was sick and you tended me, I was in prison and you visited me.'

Then the righteous will reply, 'Lord, when did we see you hungry and feed you, thirsty and gave you a drink, a stranger and help you, naked and clothe you, or in prison and visit you?'

The King will reply, 'Whatever you did for one of these brothers of mine, you did it for me.'

Then the King will say to those on his left, 'Away with you, cursed ones, into the fires prepared for the devil and his demons since the world's foundation. For I was hungry and you didn't feed me, I was thirsty and you didn't give me a drink, I was a stranger and you didn't invite me in, I was naked and you didn't clothe me, I was sick and you didn't tend me, I was in prison and you didn't visit me.'

Then the unrighteous will reply, 'Lord, when did we see you hungry and not feed you, thirsty and not give you a drink, a stranger and not help you, naked and not clothe you, or in prison and not visit you?'

The King will reply, 'Whatever you did not do for one of these brothers of mine, you didn't do it for me.'

Then the unrighteous replied, 'Wait a second, you said brothers! There are no hungry, thirsty, or naked people in my church otherwise I would have done something.'

Jesus replied, 'Good point! You may join the others.'

Thus, they shall all be herded to eternal life.

Lk 16:19-31
The Rich Man and Lazarus

There once was a rich man who was splendidly dressed and lived in luxury every day. A poor, diseased beggar named Lazarus was laid at his door. He longed to eat whatever might fall from the rich man's table, and the dogs would come and lick his open sores.

Then the beggar died and was carried by the angels to be with Abraham. The rich man also died and was buried. He ended up in hell in torment where he looked up and saw Abraham in the distance with Lazarus by his side.

He called out, 'Father Abraham, have mercy. Send Lazarus to me to dip his finger in water and cool my tongue, because I am in agony in this fire.'

But Abraham said, 'Son, remember that during your life you had everything whereas Lazarus had nothing. Now he is comforted even as you are in torment. Besides, there is a vast chasm separating us so that no one can go from here to you even if they wanted to, nor can anyone cross from there to us.'

The rich man said, 'Then send Lazarus to my father's house, for I have five brothers. Let him warn them about this place of torment so that they won't join me here.'

But Abraham replied, 'They have the Scriptures which warn them repeatedly. They can read them any time they want to.'

'No Father Abraham, if someone came back from the dead then my brothers would repent.'

Abraham replied, 'Good point! When all else fails, sending someone back from the dead will convince people, in the same way that everyone who saw Jesus perform miracles repented and believed he was the Messiah.'

Lk 12:16-21

The Rich Fool

A certain man had a vision of a bigger harvest. He told many others of his great vision and raised funds to build a huge barn ready for the harvest.

However, the barn remained empty as nobody actually sowed seed or harvested the crops.

God said to him, 'Well done! This empty barn will remain as a legacy of your great vision for years to come.'

This is how it will be for anyone who dreams dreams, but doesn't walk the walk.

Mt 13:44
The Hidden Treasure

The Kingdom of Heaven is like treasure on display in the Holy Temple that can only be seen by those who know they are most worthy. It would never be hidden in a field! After all, there would be the real danger that it might be stumbled upon by any old person.

Mt 21:28-32
The Two Sons

Jesus said, "What do you think about this?

A man had two sons. He went to the first and said, 'Son, go and work in the vineyard today.'

The son answered, 'I won't.' However, he changed his mind later on and went.

Then the father went to the other son and said, 'You go!' He answered, "Yes sir, I will.' But he never went.

Which of the two sons most pleased the father?"

"The first one," they answered.

Jesus said, "Wrong! The first one was rude right to the father's face, whereas the second one said 'sir' which shows great respect. It doesn't matter what his real intentions were. It's more important to say what you think will please others even if you do not go and do them. Similarly, as long as you speak to God in reverent terms on Sunday it does not matter what you do with the rest of your week."

Lk 10:25-37
The Good Samaritan 2

Jesus replied, "There once was a man travelling from Jerusalem to Jericho who was attacked by robbers. They beat him, stripped him of his clothes and money then left him lying half dead beside the road.

Everyone knows that road is notorious for bandits. That man was foolish for going down that road on his own. Nobody in their right mind would do that, and so he deserved all that he got."

Mt 25:14-30; Lk 19:11-27
Parable of the Talents

"The Kingdom of heaven is like a man going on a journey who called his servants together and entrusted his wealth to them. To the first, he gave five talents, to the second, two and the third, one talent, each in proportion to his ability. Then he left on his journey.

The first servant immediately invested his five talents and gained five more. The second servant gained two talents more. But the last servant dug a hole in the ground and buried his master's money for safekeeping.

After a long time, their master returned from his trip and called them to account for his investment. The first servant who had received five talents showed his master how he had obtained five more. His master praised him, 'Well done good and faithful servant! You have been faithful with a few things so now I will entrust you with much more. Come and share your master's joy!'

The second servant who had received the two talents showed his master how he had obtained two more. His master also praised him, 'Well done good and faithful servant! You have been faithful with a few things so now I will entrust you with much more. Come and share your master's joy!'

Then the last servant who had received one talent stood in front of his master and said, 'I saw that there was no point in investing what I had been given. After all, the others had been given far more than me. So, I didn't bother."

The master agreed. 'Yeah, you had a bum deal in life, so I totally see where you're coming from. In fact, you should be benefitting from the other servants' investments rather than doing anything with the little you've been given.

Take half of the first man's talents and give it to this servant who only has one. For whoever has invested well shall see his fruits given to whoever remains unfruitful.'"

Mt 18:12-14; Lk 15:4-7
The Lost Sheep 2

What do you think? If a man has one hundred sheep and loses one of them, does he not go and buy two more sheep to replace it.

After all there's plenty more where that one came from.

In the same way, your Father in heaven can easily find other people to replace you if you go wandering off.

Mt 13:1-23; Mk 4:1-20; Lk 8:1-15
Parable of the Sower

A farmer went out to his field to sow seed. But then, he noticed a nearby path and realised that birds might eat the seed that landed there. He also saw a rocky spot and realised that seeds would struggle to grow there. Finally, he saw that weeds were growing in the field, and he knew that they would choke anything that tried to grow there.

There was just too much that could go wrong if he sowed his seed!

So, he realised the safest thing to do was to keep the seed in the bag. Although it would never produce a crop, it would also never experience anything going wrong.

Mt 13:45-46
The Pearl of Great Price 2

The Kingdom of Heaven is like a merchant looking for fine jewellery. When he found an exquisite pearl of great value, he immediately inquired about it.

The vendor responded, "This beautiful pearl is the biggest of its kind in all the land."

The merchant's eyes grew wide as he beheld its rare beauty. And he knew he had to own it, even if it cost everything he had.

The vendor continued, "Do you know how such a thing of beauty is formed?"

The merchant shook his head.

The vendor continued, "Well it begins when the smallest grain of dirt gets in an oyster. That grain irritates it and in response, the oyster forms a beautiful coating around it."

"So you mean to say that this expensive pearl has a grain of dirt in its centre?"

"Absolutely!" the vendor responded, "All pearls do."

"Well then, it appears I was clearly wrong. How could I have ever thought it was beautiful? And I think you are greatly mistaken to think that anyone would pay such a price for coated dirt! Good day to you, sir!"

The merchant walked away, and the vendor was shocked, unable to comprehend the merchant's dismissal of the exquisite pearl's value just because of its humble beginnings.

Mt 18:21-35
The Unforgiving Servant

Then Peter came to Jesus and asked, "Master, how many times should I forgive my brother who sins against me? The other rabbis say three times."

Jesus replied, "The Kingdom of Heaven is like a king who decided to settle accounts with his servants. One of his servants who was brought before him owed seven billion dollars. The king grabbed him by the throat and demanded, 'Pay back what you owe me!'

As the servant couldn't possibly pay his debt, the king ordered the man, his wife, children, and all his belongings to be sold to repay the debt.

"The man threw himself at the king's feet and begged, 'Be patient with me, and I'll pay it all back.'

But the king refused and had the servant tortured by the jailers until he had paid back every last penny.

So too should you never forgive. As my Heavenly Father holds a grudge and takes your sin and puts it on display for all to see, do likewise to those who have sinned against you."

Mt 22:10-14

The Wedding Garment

The king said to his servants, 'The wedding banquet is ready, but those I invited weren't worthy. Therefore, go to the street corners and invite everybody you see.' So, the servants brought in anyone they could find; the good, the bad, and the ugly, until the wedding hall was full to the brim.

But when the King entered the hall, he noticed a man who wasn't wearing the wedding clothes provided for him. However, the king was frightened of being seen as judgemental and so he said nothing. Similarly, all the other guests kept quiet. The man became emboldened and began to shout at anyone who glanced his way, 'What are you staring at?' And so, the king's son and his bride were dishonoured on their wedding day.

For few are chosen and many won't say anything from the fear of offending those who aren't.

Mt 25:14-30; Lk 19:11-27
Parable of the Talents 2

"The Kingdom of heaven is like a man going on a journey who called his servants together and entrusted his wealth to them. To the first, he gave five talents, to the second, two and the third, one talent, each in proportion to his ability. Then he left on his journey.

The first servant immediately invested his five talents and gained three more. The second servant gained two talents more, and the third servant gained one talent more.

After a long time, their master returned from his trip and called them to account for his investment. The third servant, who had received one talent, showed his master how he had obtained one more. His master praised him, 'Well done good and faithful servant! You have been faithful with one thing so now I will entrust you with much more. Come and share your master's joy!'

The second servant, who had received the two talents, showed his master how he had obtained two more. His master also praised him, 'Well done good and faithful servant! You have been faithful with a few things so now I will entrust you with much more. Come and share your master's joy!'

Then the first servant who had received the five talents showed his master how he had obtained three more. His master asked, 'Is that all?' The first servant replied, 'Well the second servant produced two more, and the third servant produced only one more, so clearly I'm still the highest achiever.'

The master replied, 'Well I suppose if you put it like that then I see you have produced the greatest amount. It's all about quantity, after all, and not making full use of what you've been entrusted with. As to those who have been given much, only slightly more will be required of them.'"

Lk 15:11-32
The Prodigal Son 2

A mother had two sons. The youngest said to her, 'Give me my share of the estate now, rather than making me wait until you die.' And so, with a broken heart, the mother agreed and divided her property between them.

Soon after, the younger son packed all he had and set off for a distant country. There he squandered his money in wild living until it was all gone. At that time, there was a great famine. But before her son began to be in need, his mother began sending him regular food parcels.

And so, the boy never had to face the consequences of his actions, nor did he end up feeding pigs. He never did come to his senses. Despite sending assurances that he would come home and visit, he remained in that far away land, living an unrepentant life.

Lk 18:1-8
The Persistent Widow 2

Jesus told his disciples a parable to show the need to be persistent in prayer and never quit. He said, "There was a judge in a town who did not fear God nor did he care for people. A widow in that town kept bothering him, 'Grant me justice against my adversary.' At first, the judge ignored her, but then she posted her plight on Facebook and asked for prayer. Soon she had over a 1000 likes and shares.

'I might not fear God nor care for people, but if I don't give this woman justice, this post will go viral!'"

Then Jesus said, "If an evil judge can change his mind because of social media, don't you think God will give justice to his chosen people who continue to post their prayer requests online?

He won't put them off, He will answer them as soon as they go viral. But the question is; will I find such persistent posting when I return?"

Lk 16:1-12
The Shrewd Manager

Jesus told this story to his disciples, "There was a rich man who had a manager who handled his affairs. However, he heard reports that the manager was lining his own pockets. So he summoned him and asked, 'What's this I hear about you? You're sacked, and I want a complete audit of your books.'

The manager said to himself, 'What am I to do now? I'm not strong enough for manual labour, and I'm too proud to beg. Wait! I know what to do to ensure that I have friends to support me after I've lost my job.'

So he summoned each of his master's debtors. To the first he asked, 'How much do you owe my master?'

The man replied, '900 gallons of olive oil.'

The manager said, 'Let's change your bill to only half as much.'

The man refused, 'That's just dishonest. You're lucky I don't report this to your master.'

The manager was taken aback, but undeterred he tried with the next debtor and asked, 'And how much do you owe?'

The man replied, 'A 1,000 bushels of wheat.'

The manager said, 'Let's change your bill to only 800.'

The man was shocked, 'Whilst your master is known for being a kind and generous man, I suspect he is unaware of your dealings here. The Torah is clear that stealing is wrong.'

The manager cursed, he had not counted on people being honest. Now despite his best efforts, he had only further proved his reputation for dishonesty.

Mt 13:24-30, 36-43
The Wheat and the Tares 2

Jesus told them this parable, "The Kingdom of Heaven is like a man who sowed good seed in his field. While he slept, his enemy came and sowed tares in the middle of the corn. When the good seed grew, so did the weeds.

The servants saw this and came to him and said, 'Sir, wasn't that good seed that you sowed in the field? Where did all the weeds come from?'

He answered, 'An enemy has done this.'

They responded, 'Shall we pull them up?'

'Only if you're very careful, because tares look very similar and so it will be easy to pull up the wheat by mistake.'

So, the servants made sure only to pull up the plants if they read they were tares from the blogs and posted by other farmers on social media about the crop. At least that saved them the bother of having to check things thoroughly for themselves.

Mt 13:31-32; Mk 4:30-32; Lk 13:18-19
Parable of the Mustard Seed

The Kingdom of Heaven is like a mustard seed that a man planted. Over time it grew into the biggest of all trees. Its poisonous seeds allowed no bird to eat them and its spiky branches allowed no bird to shelter there.

Mt:21:33-44; Mk 12:1-12; Lk 20:9-18
The Wicked Tenants

Jesus spoke to them in parables. "A man planted a vineyard. He put a wall around it, dug a pit for the winepress, and built a watchman's tower. Then he and his son tended the vineyard themselves. The man could have leased it to tenants, but he didn't trust that the tenants would have done as good a job as he and his son. Furthermore, he reasoned, the tenants might steal the crop from him at harvest time or even do something worse. This way was much safer, and so he collected a great harvest."

Lk 10:25-37
The Good Samaritan 3

Jesus replied, "There once was a man travelling from Jerusalem to Jericho who was attacked by robbers. They beat him, stripped him of his clothes and money, then left him lying half dead beside the road.

Luckily, an atheist happened to be going down the same road. When he saw the man he sighed, 'That's just the way the world is.' But as it wasn't his problem, the atheist averted his eyes, crossed to the other side, and walked past.

So too, an agnostic came by. He saw the man and felt guilty that he didn't stop as he crossed to the other side and continued on. He berated himself all the way to Jericho.

Then a Christian came upon the man, saw him there, and had compassion on him. 'I'm so glad I give money to a charity that helps the unfortunate.' He too carried on.

Which of these three would you say was a neighbour to the man attacked by robbers?"

The expert in the law replied, "The one who gave to charity."

Jesus replied, "Go and do likewise."

Mt 25:31-46
The Sheep and the Goats 2

When the Son of Man comes in all his blazing glory together with his angels, he shall sit on his glorious throne. And all the nations shall be gathered before him and he shall separate the people as a shepherd separates the sheep from the goats, putting the sheep to his right and goats to his left.

But unlike the Middle Eastern sheep and goats, these were like the ones in the West, and as such, they were easy to tell apart. Everyone already knew who were the holy ones and who were the sinners.

Then the King will say to those on his right, 'Come, blessed of my Father, take your inheritance - the Kingdom prepared for you from the world's foundation. For you lived separately from the world in your Christian bubble. You subscribed to God TV, you purchased only Christian music and watched only Christian movies. I was particularly impressed when you watched those movies, as some of them were truly terrible.'

Then the righteous will reply, 'Lord, we already knew that we were holy and deserving of your blessing for we kept apart from non-Christians, trolled atheists and listened to only

Christian music and sermons. We also endured those terrible Christian movies.'

Then the King will say to those on his left, 'Away with you, cursed ones, into the fires prepared for the devil and his demons since the world's foundation. For you never listened to God TV, you watched movies from Hollywood, and listened to secular music. You also smoked, drank alcohol, wore clothes that were inappropriate, and got tattoos and piercings.'

Then the unrighteous will reply, 'Lord, we already knew that we were destined for hell, the Christians who stand on corners and yell at us told us so. We didn't listen to God TV nor Christian music. We did smoke, drink, wear inappropriate clothes, we did get tattoos and piercings. But, you have to admit that we made the right choice about not watching those Christian movies.'

The King will reply, 'OK, I'll let you off the movies, but the rest of the stuff is just out and out sinful and can't be redeemed.'

Then they shall be herded to their eternal punishment, but the righteous to eternal life.

Perfect Parables

What would it be like if all the characters in the parables made the right choices?

Lk 16:1-12
The Shrewd Manager

Jesus told this story to his disciples, "There was a rich man who had a manager who handled his affairs. However, he heard reports that the manager was lining his own pockets. So, he summoned him and asked, 'What's this I hear about you? You're sacked and I want a complete audit of your books!'

"The manager said to himself, 'What am I to do now? I know, I shall come clean and tell all and seek to make amends.'

"He fell on his knees before his master, 'Here is the complete list of all the money I have cheated you out of,' As he pointed to a bag of gold he had with him, the manager admitted, 'And this is everything I have left of it. I know I've blown it here and I will seek employment elsewhere so I can pay you back four times the amount still outstanding.'

"His master was sceptical of the manager's sudden change of heart, but he decided to give him another chance.

"Over time, the manager proved his transformation to be real and lasting. The rich man not only got his money back, but he got a better manager than he ever had before. The master realised that salvation had come to his house and entrusted the servant with more of his property."

Lk 16:19-31
The Rich Man and Lazarus

There once was a rich man who was splendidly dressed and lived in luxury every day. A poor, diseased beggar named Lazarus was laid at his door. When the rich man was told of Lazarus, he had his servants bring him in, treat his sores and prepare a guest room for him

Each day the rich man dined with Lazarus where they discussed the coming Kingdom.

Then Lazarus and the rich man both died and were carried by the angels to be with Abraham sharing the joy of Paradise together.

Mt 22:10-14
The Wedding Garment

The king said to his servants, 'The wedding banquet is ready, but those I invited weren't worthy. Therefore, go to the street corners and invite everybody you see.' So, the servants brought in anyone they could find; the good, the bad, and the ugly, until the wedding hall was full to the brim.

As most of them had only the clothes on their backs, wedding clothes were provided for them. The guests were overcome by the graciousness of the host, and they gladly put the fine garments on. They felt like a million dollars.

When the King entered the hall, he saw they were all dressed in honour of his son's wedding and was delighted. 'Let the wedding begin!' he announced.

Mt 25:1-13
The Ten Virgins

The Kingdom of Heaven is like ten girls who took their lamps and went out to meet the bridegroom. All of them were wise and took oil in their lamps reservoir. For they had matured through the spiritual disciplines and invested their time and hearts into a relationship with the Father.

Now the bridegroom was taking his time in his wedding procession, and they all grew drowsy and fell asleep. But at midnight there was a shout, 'Here comes the bridegroom! Come out to meet him!'

Then all those girls awoke and trimmed their lamps and joined the wedding procession as it danced its way into the wedding banquet.

Pointless Parables

Just for a little light hearted fun...

Mt 22:1-14; Lk 14:15-24
The Great Banquet

Once, there was a man who prepared a great banquet and then sent out many invitations. It was going to be one of the murder mystery suppers but the real mystery was why no one showed up.

Lk 10:25-37
The Good Samaritan

Jesus replied, "There once was a man travelling from Jerusalem to Jericho who fell into the hands of robbers."

"They must have had big hands," the expert in the law thought.

Mt 13:44
The Hidden Treasure

The Kingdom of Heaven is like treasure hidden in a field. When a man found it, he said, 'Found you! Now it's my turn to hide.'

Mt 13:47-50
Parable of the Net

The Kingdom of Heaven is like a net cast into the sea that caught all kinds of things. But it didn't catch any birds. That's because they don't live underwater.

Mt:21:33-44; Mk 12:1-12; Lk 20:9-18
The Wicked Tenants

Jesus spoke to them in parables. "A man planted a vineyard. He put a wall around it, dug a pit for the winepress, and built a watchman's tower. Then he leased it to some tenant farmers and went away. At harvest time, he sent a servant to collect his share of the crop.

The tenants said, 'No!'

The servant replied, 'Please.'

The tenants changed their minds and said, 'oh alright then.'"

The L^OST Parables

Allegorical tales that speak straight to the heart.

The Cyst of Shame

It was Emily's habit to see her doctor at least once a week where she would have a routine check-up.

"Good to see you again, Emily. How are you doing?" he would ask.

"Oh, I'm fine," she would always reply, "What I really want to talk to you this week is about my friend Agnes. She's struggling with…"

And so each time she would ask for the doctor's help for someone else.

Emily missed several of her regular appointments one week and when she eventually returned her doctor enquired, "Emily, it's so good to see you. I wondered where you'd been."

Emily brushed off his concern, "I'm fine."

"Where were you for the last week?" he probed.

"I was…umm…" her voice dropped to a whisper, "not feeling well."

"But Emily, that's precisely the time you need to see me!" he implored.

Emily shifted uncomfortably in her seat and then quickly pressed on, "This week I'd really like it if you could help my friend Rachael…"

Over the next few months, Emily's attendance grew even more erratic. Her face became pinched in pain, and she slowly developed a hunch on one shoulder. Eventually, she got to the point where she could take it no longer.

"I don't mean to be a bother, but I am… umm not feeling well."

"I know, Emily." Her doctor asked gently. "Why don't you let me look at that lump on your shoulder,"

Emily's face went white with shock, "How did you…?" she trailed off.

Then she blurted, "I…I…I can't." and fled the room in tears.

It was some time later before Emily booked another appointment. The unbearable pain made her desperate.

"I wondered if you might give me something for this," She pointed to the growing lump on her shoulder.

"Well I'll need to take a look at it before I can make a diagnosis."

Emily was crestfallen. She had hoped that he would prescribe something without actually examining her. She slowly removed her cardigan and exposed a nasty cyst. After a brief examination, the doctor said seriously, "Emily, it's obvious this growth is cancerous and..."

Emily stood upright, "I knew this would happen – that's why I never wanted to talk about it!"

Before the doctor could respond, Emily stormed out of his office.

Months went by before Emily set foot in the door again. Her eyes were sunken in her ashen face.

"It's taken me a while to come to terms with what you said. But you're right." She couldn't bring herself to look at him directly as she conceded, "I am a cancerous person but if it's okay with you, I'd still like to come and ask you to help others."

Incredulity left her doctor slack-jawed, "Emily!" His voice softened. "You misunderstood me. The reason I told you what was wrong with your shoulder was so you'd give me permission to remove it."

"Remove it?"

"Yes, it needs to be removed as soon as possible."

"But... but, you can't do that!" she stammered, "It's...it's part of me!"

"You are more than this cancerous growth – this cyst isn't who you are."

Fear filled her eyes, "But who will I be when it is gone?"

"You will be the healthy you I've always wanted to help you become."

Emily surrendered to his wisdom and consented to the operation. The first thing she saw when she came to in the recovery room was the triumphant grin of her doctor. "I'm pleased to say that we have removed all of the cancerous tissue." He held a jar aloft containing the growth.

"Thank you so much," said Emily. She snatched the jar, took the cyst out and placed it back on her shoulder, sighing with relief.

"Emily, do you trust me?"

"Yes."

"Then let me burn it. Then you can be free of this forever."

Emily clutched the cyst protectively. On one hand, it was clear the cyst was no longer part of her, but on the other hand, she was drawn to it - finding an odd sense of comfort and identity in its familiar presence.

She thought about it for a long time before she made the bravest choice of her life and surrendered the cyst to her doctor who promptly threw the vile cancer into the incinerator. Which is the only place such things belong.

For a while afterwards Emily walked with a hunch as if she still had the cyst. But bit by bit, over time, she began to walk tall in who she really was. Although she felt free in many ways, she was embarrassed about the scars on her shoulder which she always kept covered.

"Will these ever heal?" she asked her doctor one day.

"They have healed." he replied.

"But the scars…"

"What about them?"

For the first time, Emily noticed the horrendous scars on both of his hands as her doctor gestured to her own scars. She wondered why she had not noticed them before.

"How….?"

"Scars are signs of victory not defeat. They show the sacrifices that were made to bring wholeness."

Seeing the wisdom in what her doctor said, Emily eventually stopped hiding her scars and proudly displayed them as part of her journey. Her brave vulnerability had the strangest effect on others. Yes, there were some who tried to project their own shame on her. However, there were many more who asked how she got those scars. And as she shared her story, they sheepishly admitted they had been struggling with such growths as well.

Her scars became a symbol of hope, and many received healing as they took her advice and sought out the doctor for themselves.

"By his wounds we are healed" Isa 53:5b

Other "Lost Parables" are available as eBooks on Amazon with illustrations. Suitable for use in all age church services, family devotions, Sunday school or for reading to your children or to yourself.

N⊘T the Beginning

A clever section title that makes it sound like it's more important than 'all the stuff that goes at the end of a book'...

Get Bonus Content

Subscribers to my mailing list will receive a free eBook or audiobook of *"Not the Parable of the Lost Sheep"* and, if you stick around you'll also receive *"Not the Parable of the Rich Fool"*. Twenty satirical takes on this parable not available anywhere else.

www.johnspencerwrites.com/signup

In addition you'll also receive:

- an email every Friday(ish) chock full of the week's memes I put out on social media
- details of the monthly competitions where you can win signed copies of my books
- notifications of all promotional deals on my books
- opportunities to beta read and receive free review copies
- the satisfaction of making John feel loved and wanted.

Alternatively, if you'd just like to know when I'm releasing new books then feel free to sign up, grab the first freebie, unsubscribe, then follow me on Amazon, Goodreads or BookBub.

Feedback

This is the part of the book where the self-publishing author puts their dignity to one side and begs for reviews.

Since you clearly don't want me to debase myself in such a way, why don't you just head over to Amazon or Goodreads and scribble a short heartfelt review there.

That way you can skip the next paragraph and move onto the next part where I mention I've written some other books.

Please, please, please write a review. I'll be your bestest friend. OK, maybe that last bit puts you right off. So pretty please with a cherry on top. Your review will make all the difference to my ego, I mean to my ability to reach others with this message of funniness. Think of all the fluffy kitties whose lives will be helped by your review.

About the Author

John was born at a very young age with his umbilical cord wrapped around his neck. At first, it appeared that no lasting damage had been done, but as he grew it became clear that his sense of humour had been damaged irreparably.

Not even Bible College, counselling, and prayer ministry has been able to rectify things, so John eagerly awaits the new creation where his humour will be perfected.

John also trained as a teacher at Oxford University, but despite this he still refers to himself in the third person. Whilst there, he performed stand-up comedy as part of the Oxford Revue but got tired and has been sitting down at his desk to perform his humour ever since.

So now, when he's not wrestling with work-life balance or literally wrestling with his four children, he's wrestling with writing funny words on a page in his cramped study.

John lives with his family near Oxford, England where daily he wonders how his wife still finds the same jokes funny after more than 20 years of marriage.

Keep in touch

Mailing list – did I mention that you can sign up and receive bonus eBooks/audiobooks? Just thought I'd remind you. You know, just in case.

Amazon, Goodreads and Bookbub

These will let you know when I publish new books.

Social media

I post memes daily at **Not the Bible** on **Facebook, Twitter,** and **Pinterest**. I'm most active on **Twitter** exchanging banter with the rest of the Christian anon gang.

And you're least likely to see my humorous memes on Facebook unless you choose "See First" under the "Liked" menu on my page. If the thought of this makes you sad, then you know what to do.

Web

I blog occasionally at www.johnspencerwrites.com

And I write Christian satirical news at www.saltycee.com

Other books by the Author

After reading this book you might be tempted to check out my earlier books to see if I was funnier before I ran out of ideas.

If not, then why not think of your purchase as helping keep me off of the streets where my humour could cause some serious harm to innocent bystanders.

Not the Bible Titles

Alternative takes on the original parables to snap us out of our over-familiarity and open our eyes to the truth of the Gospel.

Not the Parables of Jesus

More Not the Parables of Jesus

Not the Parable of the Good Samaritan

Not the Parable of the Lost Sheep *(free for subscribers)*

Not the Parable of the Rich Fool *(subscribers only)*

Not the Christmas Story Vol 1*(with devotional)*

Christian Parody Titles

Not the Love Dare
Because everyone needs some biblical help to justify their annoying habits to their spouse

Not the Christmas Story: A Comedic Christmas Caper
"Fear not: for, behold, I bring you good tidings of great laughter, which shall be to all purchasers of this book."

Christian Satirical News Titles

The Best of the Salty Cee Vol 1
News Satire more salty than the Dead Sea.

Lost Parable Series

Short allegorical tales available as ebooks with illustrations for the young and the young at heart.

The Donkey and the King

Ana and the Prince

The Princess and the Crocodile

Satirical Self-Publishing titles

Get 1000 readers for your self-published book
Love it or hate it, it's the Marmite of marketing books.

And finally...

Well I guess it's all over.

As I really did scrape the barrel of ideas for this book.

So I'm a little confused why you're still reading.

It's like scrolling on social media hoping there will be something better.

But there never is.

So you just end up regretting wasting your time when you could have done something more useful instead.

Like writing a review.

www.ingramcontent.com/pod-product-compliance
Lightning Source LLC
Chambersburg PA
CBHW071010080526
44587CB00015B/2411